W9-AWL-457

CANTERBURY

Contents

Maps

Information panels

OPPOSITE **The magnificent Christ Church Gate into the Cathedral**

CANTERBURY

More than three million visitors come to Canterbury every year to see its spectacular Cathedral and experience the rare flavour of its ancient streets and buildings. As they explore the byways of the city, the Cathedral's towers and pinnacles are often in view – Canterbury was where Christianity gained its foothold on English soil 1,400 years ago when St Augustine arrived and the present Cathedral stands on the foundations of the church founded by him in 597. Six hundred years later, this was also where Archbishop Thomas Becket was struck down

Sometime in the 6th century, Canterbury emerged with a new name, Cantwarabyrig – 'the township of the men of Kent'. In 561 Ethelbert became King of Kent, and although only a boy at the time – and a pagan – he proved to be a worthy monarch and ruled for 56 years, steadily expanding the realm. He seems to have adopted Cantwarabyrig as capital soon after coming to the throne, and when he married Bertha, a Frankish princess, they lived at his palace there. Bertha was Christian and made it a condition of marriage that her faith should be tolerated. She worshipped in St Martin's, a small church on the outskirts of the city which had been founded in Roman times. When Augustine landed in Kent on his mission to re-convert England, Bertha was able to persuade her husband to meet the emissary from Rome and treat him generously. Ethelbert became one of Augustine's first converts and gave him land for both a Cathedral and an abbey at Canterbury.

St Augustine's Saxon Cathedral lasted for almost 400 years before being burned down in 1067. For much of this time, the citizens of Canterbury lived in fear of invasion as the richly-endowed Cathedral and neighbouring abbey held great treasures of interest to looters. In 839 and 850, Vikings sacked the city and its citizens had to save their lives by paying Danegelt (ransom money). In 1011 Canterbury was besieged for 20 days before being betrayed by the Prior of St Augustine's Abbey who set fire to houses close to the defences. A massacre followed with Archbishop Elphege heroically offering his own life in order to save the lives of children. Sadly, his gesture was fruitless, and it is said that 8,000 of those who sheltered in the city were slain or sold into slavery – only 800 survived.

After their invasion in 1066, the Normans speedily introduced bureaucracy and organisation, placing their own people in positions of power and influence. One of these, Lanfranc, was appointed Archbishop of Canterbury in 1070 and was dismayed on arrival to find that his Cathedral had been destroyed by fire three years earlier. A very efficient organiser, within seven years he had built a new church together with new living quarters in the monastery attached to the Cathedral.

Building was going on elsewhere in the city too, notably in its south-east quarter, where an imposing castle was

ABOVE **Canterbury Castle, built c.1120, was captured by the French Dauphin in 1216 and by Wat Tyler's rebels in 1381.**

begun in *c.*1100. Its centrepiece is the great keep, the fifth largest in England and one of the earliest to be built of stone – its walls are 8ft (2.5m) thick. The only action the castle ever saw was in 1216 when it surrendered to the French without an arrow being fired or any boiling liquid poured on to the besiegers' heads.

The murder of Archbishop Thomas Becket in his Cathedral in 1170 (see pp.22-3) was the bloody climax of a political struggle between church and state. Becket's shrine became the most popular place of pilgrimage in Christendom and brought immense wealth to the archbishopric and to the city of Canterbury. Vast lodging houses were built to accommodate the pilgrims, the Chequer of Hope in Mercery Lane could sleep 600 guests even though it only had 100 (very large) beds!

In the 14th and 15th centuries, the city walls were rebuilt, faithfully following the line of the Roman defences and sometimes incorporating their masonry.

West Gate, the most impressive of the city's eight gates, was designed by Henry Yevele (the master mason of the Cathedral nave) for Archbishop Sudbury in 1380. The gate was still being built when Wat Tyler led his rebels into the city in 1381 and looted the archbishop's palace, burned civic documents and set free prisoners. However, it proved more formidable to the rebels who came to the city in 1450. Four thousand Yorkists, under the Irishman, Jack Cade, turned away from the city after being denied entry by the mayor.

Canterbury's fortunes changed abruptly after 1538 when Henry VIII closed all monasteries and abbeys. Both of the abbeys in the city – Christ Church (attached to the Cathedral) and St Augustine's – were 'dissolved' and their wealth added to the royal treasury. Becket's shrine, encrusted with gold and precious stones, was dismantled and the bones found within it were burned. It yielded 20 wagon-loads of gold and silver for the king. Becket was declared a traitor and pilgrims ceased to visit the city, abruptly cutting off its main source of income.

Fortunately at almost the same time, Huguenot refugees from Flanders began to settle in the city,

LEFT **West Gate from St Dunstan's, 1828. Medieval travellers tried to beat the curfew when the city gates closed. If they found themselves locked out, they would have to stay at an inn in St Dunstan's.**

ABOVE **Almost half of the original circumference of the city walls survives extending from Northgate to the Norman castle.**

Geoffrey Chaucer's pilgrims came to Canterbury in holiday mood, obviously enjoying themselves, perhaps because they knew how easy it was to buy an indulgence which would pardon their sins. Pilgrims travelled to Canterbury from all over Christendom chiefly to see the shrine of the martyr St Thomas Becket, but they would also be shown further relics in the Cathedral – among them the arms of 11 saints and the heads of three others!

bringing new skills and introducing high-quality textile industries. Although they fled back to the continent on the accession of the Catholic Queen Mary in 1553, they returned to England five years later when the Protestant faith was restored by Elizabeth I.

The beginning of the 17th century saw a modest recovery in Canterbury's fortunes. The Huguenot refugees were actively establishing industry, and apart from weaving silk and wool there were silversmiths, brewers, papermakers and dentists from the Low Countries. At the height of the immigration they almost outnumbered native Englishmen in Canterbury, although they were not allowed to own property at first.

When Civil War broke out in 1642, most of Cromwell's support in Canterbury came from the poorer inhabitants. A detachment of Roundheads occupied the city and pulled down the statue of Christ from its central position in Christ Church Gate. The niche remained empty for 350 years until the present figure (by Klaus Ringwald) was put up in 1992. In contrast the medieval glass smashed down from the glorious windows of the Cathedral by a

ABOVE **The Weavers' Houses on the High Street overlook Eastbridge.**

LEFT **The statue of Christ Blessing in the central niche of Christ Church Gate is by Klaus Ringwald and was installed in 1992.**

fanatical Puritan minister, 'Blue Dick' Culmer, could never be adequately replaced, nor could the hundreds of exquisitely carved figures of saints and angels which also suffered.

Canterbury soon became disillusioned with Puritanism and in 1647 a mob turned on the mayor and acclaimed King Charles after the mayor had attempted to ban the celebration of Christmas. This boisterous uprising was suppressed, but unrest broke out again in the following year before the Royalists were routed at the Battle of Maidstone by General Fairfax. In 1651 Canterbury was ardently Parliamentarian when Cromwell visited the city.

Puritan rule ended in Canterbury in 1659 with a mob hanging the governor of the city from a window of the West Gate. In 1660 Charles II rode in triumph through the city on his return from exile to his coronation at Westminster.

Christopher Marlowe was born in Canterbury in 1564 and baptized in St George's Church. The son of a shoemaker, he was educated at King's School, Canterbury and Corpus Christi College, Cambridge. As a boy he watched strolling players perform plays in the courtyards of Canterbury inns. He joined the Earl of Nottingham's company of actors in London in 1587, for whom he wrote a series of plays, including *Tamburlaine the Great*. A master of blank verse, he may have collaborated with Shakespeare in his early plays and also translated the Roman poets Ovid and Lucan. He was probably involved in espionage for the government, and died in suspicious circumstances at an inn at Deptford in 1593. The engraving above shows Doctor Faustus conjuring the devil.

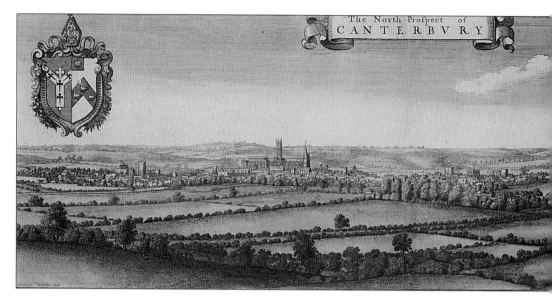

ABOVE **An 18th-century panorama of Canterbury from the north.**

BELOW **This print from the *Illustrated London News* shows the railway line to Dover in 1846 and the level crossing in St Dunstan's which then, as now, thwarted road traffic.**

On visiting Canterbury in the 18th century, Daniel Defoe commented that the city's antiquity was its greatest beauty, but he saw the city before the Commission for Paving, which first met in 1787, widened streets and knocked down most of the city gates so that traffic could flow more freely. Some of Canterbury's medieval character was lost in these 'improvements', which made the frontages of old buildings more uniform by removing projections such as bay windows, forecourts and porches, the features which gave the street scenes their pictorial appeal. By

this time, Canterbury had become settled in its role as county town and market centre, though most ecclesiastical business was conducted at Lambeth, and some archbishops never lived in their palace at Canterbury.

At the end of the 18th century, the threat posed by the French made Canterbury strategically important. Sprawling barracks were built to house 5,000 troops and occupied more ground than the city itself. William Cobbett, writing in 1823 (just 100 years after Defoe), found the prospect of the city utterly spoiled by 'the county of barracks' which surrounded the ancient walls.

Canterbury played an important role in the development of railways. In 1830 its first railway linked the city with the small port of Whitstable, 6 miles (9.5km) to the north, and was the first passenger railway (beating Manchester and Liverpool by 5 months), although its carriages had to be linked to stationary engines at two points in order to climb to the top of the steep-sided Blean plateau. The *Invicta* locomotive was designed by the Stephenson brothers, and provided the motive power for the

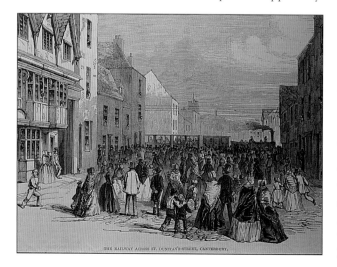

THE RAILWAY ACROSS ST. DUNSTAN'S-STREET, CANTERBURY.

fell on the roof of the Cathedral (from where brave firefighters threw them to the ground), miraculously the building itself was unscathed. Almost a quarter of the medieval city was destroyed, and today the tower of St George's Church stands among post-war buildings as a monument to its lost parish.

northern section. It is now on display at the Canterbury Heritage Museum.

Canterbury enjoyed steady, if not spectacular, growth throughout Victorian times and up until the outbreak of World War II. Its tranquillity was ended abruptly on the night of 1 June 1942 – Trinity Sunday – when German bombers attacked the city. Although 15 high-explosive bombs brought great damage to the Precincts and countless incendiaries

Even before the start of the 20th century, workers were commuting to London from Canterbury by rail. This, with the city's growth as a regional centre and the establishment of the University of Kent in 1962, meant that Canterbury grew steadily outwards, and suburban housing covered the large tracts of land formerly occupied by barracks and parade grounds. Like all the universities of the 1960s, former parkland was chosen for its site, in this case at the top of St Thomas' Hill, which gives a magnificent prospect of the city, with the Cathedral as the centrepiece. The founding of the university continues the tradition of scholarship in Canterbury, which was begun by the 7th archbishop, St Theodore of Tarsus, in the 7th century.

BELOW **The well-timbered grounds of the University of Kent at Canterbury provide a splendid vantage point from which to enjoy a view the city.**

The Cathedral and Precincts

THE NUN'S PRIEST

The approach to Canterbury Cathedral through the magnificent Christ Church Gate affords a dramatic first view of this splendid building. The gate itself was built between 1517 and 1520, less than 20 years before Henry VIII dissolved the Abbey of Christ Church, to which the Cathedral belonged. The gate's wooden doors carry the arms of Archbishop Luxon and thus date from 1660. Prince Arthur, Henry's elder brother, who died in 1502 on his honeymoon at the age of 15, sponsored the building of the gate and his shields decorate the exterior side. The side facing the Cathedral is plain. Just inside the gate there is an attractive row of timber-framed houses, but it is the Cathedral itself which attracts most attention.

The size of the Cathedral is not immediately apparent because the east end is hidden at first and the eye is irresistibly held by Bell Harry, the central tower. Dating from the late 15th century, this was the last major feature of the Cathedral to be built. It is just under 250ft (76m) high and its stone facing conceals 1½ million bricks within – at the time it was the first major building to be constructed of brick since Roman times.

BELOW The Cathedral and rooftops of Canterbury seen from the Marlowe Theatre.

ABOVE Christ Church Gate provides a magnificent entrance to the Cathedral Precincts. Its elaborate decoration with innumerable heraldic shields pays homage to the last patron of the Abbey, the young Prince Arthur, brother of Henry VIII.

ABOVE **This quaint cottage by Christ Church Gate was once the house of the gatekeeper.**

RIGHT **A breathtaking view of the nave.**

BELOW RIGHT **Look heavenwards to see the fan vaulting beneath Bell Harry tower.**

Entering the Cathedral by the porch at the western end of the nave you are immediately confronted by the splendour of soaring pillars which lead the eye heavenwards to the intricate lierne vaulting of the ceiling. This work ranks among the greatest achievements of the medieval mason, yet the nave is almost the newest part of the Cathedral. Dating from *c*.1400, it is the work of Henry Yevele, Edward III's mason who also built the nave of Westminster Abbey.

LEFT **This effigy of Henry Yevele, master mason, who worked in the Cathedral for 28 years, can be found on one of the cloister roof bosses.**

ABOVE The beautiful Chapel of Our Lady in the Undercroft.

BELOW Examples of the wonderful carvings which decorate the capitals of the Norman crypt and St Gabriel's Chapel.

To visit the oldest part of the Cathedral, the crypt, walk down the centre of the nave and follow the arrows left to climb the steps and pass the Altar of the Sword's Point in the north transept, the site of Becket's murder. Beyond this, more steps lead down into the crypt, dedicated to silence and contemplation.

The visitors' route passes by the Chapel of Our Lady, half hidden by its lacy, stone screen dating from

c.1380, into the crypt of Trinity Chapel. This dates from the rebuilding, completed at the end of the 12th century by William the Englishman. Walk round the east end and return to the earlier crypt; from this side its magnificence is more apparent. All that remains of the 1070–77 Cathedral, built by Archbishop Lanfranc, are the 22 massive columns, many of them decorated, which support the quire above. The capitals of the columns are elaborately carved with a series of amusing designs, most of which showing bizarre creatures in conflict. Less aggressive are the animals depicted playing musical instruments on the capitals in St Gabriel's Chapel. The carvings are the finest of the period in England. Another remarkable

BELOW **The 15th-century pulpitum (quire screen) is a *tour de force* with angels and heraldic shields set above carvings of six kings which replaced those of 'twelve mitred saints' knocked down at the Reformation.**

feature of the crypt is its windows, many of them displaying magnificent stained glass. Needless to say, very few crypts can boast windows, and the height of this one explains why the east end of the Cathedral is higher than the nave. The Cathedral treasury occupies the western end of the crypt.

Visitors climb the steps out of the crypt to emerge in the south transept and then climb more steps to reach the pulpitum or 'Screen of the Six Kings' which separates the quire from the nave. Its name is derived from the dominant stone figures of the kings (probably, from left to right: Henry V, Richard II, Ethelbert, Edward the Confessor, Henry IV and Henry VI). Originally the screen also depicted figures of 12 saints, all wearing mitres, but these were destroyed by

Cromwell's vandals. Before passing through the screen to the quire glance up to see the delicate fan vaulting 126ft (38m) above.

The quire was burned down in 1174, only four years after Becket's death, but his body was buried in the crypt and came to no harm. Work on a new quire began within two years of the fire, the master mason being a Frenchman, William of Sens. Unfortunately, in 1178, just as he was about to make a start on the vaulting, he fell 50ft (15m) from a wooden scaffold and injured himself so severely that he was forced to return to France. The task of completing the quire was given to a monk, another William (usually called 'the Englishman' to distinguish him from the original mason), and it is his work beyond the high altar today, with the great arches drawing in towards Trinity Chapel to enclose the space designed to hold the shrine of St Thomas Becket.

Visitors usually leave the quire and go into the north aisle to pass the

BELOW **Seen from the west end of the quire the perspective of rising columns skilfully contrives to draw the eye towards Trinity Chapel, built to contain the shrine of St Thomas Becket.**

RIGHT The Miracle Window in the north aisle of Trinity Chapel shows scenes of the miracles attributed to St Thomas Becket surrounding the image of pilgrims at his shrine in the centre.

BELOW The Black Prince (d.1376) was the eldest son of Edward III and a frequent visitor to the shrine of St Thomas Becket before his campaigns in France.

tomb of Henry IV and his queen which separates the aisle from Trinity Chapel. On the other side of the aisle, magnificent stained glass illustrates miracles attributed to St Thomas and his shrine. The chapel at the eastern end of the Cathedral is called the 'Corona' because it was here that a particularly important relic was kept, the crown of Becket's head which had been hacked off by a Norman sword. The tomb of the Black Prince, the effigy in full armour, is on the south side of Trinity Chapel, facing that of his nephew, Henry IV. The chapel dedicated to St Anselm, a little further on, has a vivid 12th-century mural, which shows (continued on p.18)

A walk in Canterbury

This walk takes in the most beautiful and memorable features of Canterbury, starting from Christ Church Gate. The time taken will depend on how long you decide to linger at the city's various fascinating attractions, but should be little more than an hour.

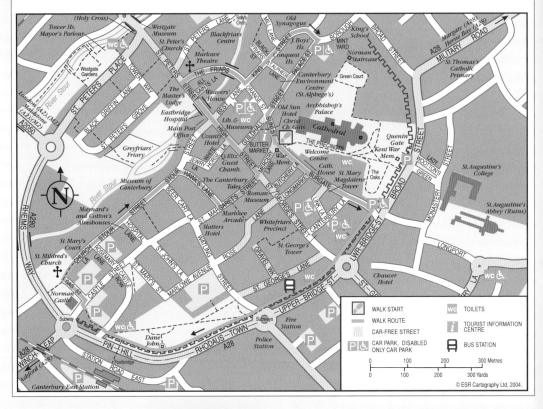

The walk starts outside **Christ Church Gate** (*right*) (p.10) – a magnificent entry into the Cathedral precincts built between 1517 and 1520. Leaving the gate, turn left past the war memorial and

walk down Burgate – this section of the city suffered the worst from bombing in 1942. Continue along Burgate to pass the tower of St Mary Magdalene church. At the end of the street turn right to follow the 'City Walls Walk' sign, keep inside the walls and pass the quaint Zoar Baptist Chapel of 1845 (*right*), which

occupies a former bastion of the walls. These defence-works were originally built by the Romans. The **medieval walls** (p.6) followed the same line and had eight gates and 21 towers. Use the underpass to cross St George's Street and then climb to the top of the walls.

The City Walls Walk crosses Watling Street, the Roman Road which entered the city here through Ridingate. Continue a little further for a good view into Dane John Gardens, with its terrace of attractive Regency houses. The gardens themselves were laid

out by Alderman James Simmons in 1790. The walls skirt round an earthen mound, **Dane John** (*left*) (p.4), an Iron Age burial-site. It was re-shaped into a cone by Alderman Simmons and his memorial is located at the top.

The City Walls Walk ends where a footbridge crosses the main road to Canterbury East station. Keep inside the walls, descend the ramp to the right and cross Castle Row to the alley by Don Jon House which leads to Castle Street and **Canterbury Castle** (pp.5, 27). Follow Gas Street, to the right of the Castle, to **St Mildred's church** (p.24).

Leaving the church, turn left into Church Lane which leads to Stour Street. Continue straight on to pass Maynard's Spittal on the right – a row of one-storey almshouses – and you come to the Poor Priests' Hospital on the left, now the **Canterbury Heritage Museum** (p.28). At the end of the hospital buildings, turn right and at the end of the lane, turn left. St Margaret's Church, housing the re-created world of **Chaucer and the Canterbury Tales** (pp.25 & 29), is on the left. Turn left into High Street and pass the **Queen Elizabeth Guest Chamber** (*above*) (p.27) on the left and the **Royal Museum and Art Gallery** (p.29) on the right. A little further on, cross the River Stour over King's Bridge. The **Old Weavers' Houses** (pp.7, 26) front the river here and **Eastbridge**

Hospital (*left*) (p.26) is opposite, on the left.

Turn right into The Friars and pass the memorial to **Christopher Marlowe** (above *right*) (p.7) and then the theatre named after him. The road takes you across the river

again, then turn left at the crossroads into King Street. Look left at the next crossroads to see the former Blackfriars monastery. The Old Synagogue is tucked away on the left just before King Street bends right to pass **Sir John Boys' House** (*below*) (p.27).

Turn right into Palace Street, which takes its name from the Archbishop's Palace, concealed behind the buildings on the left. **Conquest House** (p.27), on the right, is supposed to have been the rendezvous of Becket's murderers. St Alphege's church (*below*), now used as the Canterbury Environment Centre, is on your right, while a few doors further on is **The Tudor House** (p.27), with its grotesque decoration on the ends of supporting beams. Beaus Restaurant is on

the left before the junction. It was once called **The Mayflower Restaurant** (*below*) because it is supposed to be where Robert Cushman (p.25) contracted to hire the *Mayflower* on behalf of the Pilgrim Fathers. Bear left into Sun Street – facing you is the former **Sun Hotel** (p.26) patronized by Charles Dickens. The **Tourist Information Centre**, with shop and details of places to visit in and around Canterbury, is on the same side. Christ Church Gate is a few yards further on.

St Paul shaking off the viper. Before leaving the Cathedral glance in at St Michael's Chapel in the south transept. Known as the Warriors' Chapel because of the regimental colours which hang there, it also contains some splendid monuments.

Outside, walk along the south side of the Cathedral heading east and the sheer scale of the building becomes apparent (it is 810ft/246m long), along with the mixture of styles and

the tricks which a succession of masons used to enable the side chapels in transepts and aisles to face east. Look for the little stone projection on the outside wall of St Michael's Chapel. It houses the end of the tomb of Archbishop Stephen Langton (d.1228) who promoted the cult of St Thomas and created his shrine. When St Michael's Chapel was shortened in 1430, the Archbishop's tomb was too long, so his feet were left poking outside.

Turn westwards around the Corona at the end of the Cathedral and you will see the ruins of the infirmary built *c*.1160 for the monastery. The path beside the ruins leads through the romantically-named 'Dark Entry' into the cloisters. However, if you turn right on entering the passageway, you will emerge into Green Court, which is overlooked on three sides by the buildings of King's School. The north side of the Cathedral occupies the fourth side – the curious little arcaded tower supplied the monks with

running water from a cistern above the arcade. Close by were the monks' lavatories or 'necessarium' which could cater for 56 clients at a time, back to back. Fragments of this still survive. In the far north-west corner of Green Court is the famous Norman Staircase which leads up to the North Hall, the principal hall for the monastery's poorer guests.

ABOVE **Look for this 'dog kennel' on the south side of the Cathedral. It houses the feet of Archbishop Stephen Langton.**

ABOVE RIGHT **The ruins of the Abbey Infirmary are a picturesque feature of the Cathedral Precincts.**

LEFT **The Norman Staircase is in the far, northern, corner of Green Court. The final cistern of Prior Wibert's water supply once** occupied a chamber above the arches.

ABOVE **Mint Yard lies to the north-west of Green Court and commemorates the mint that occupied the site in Norman times.**

St Augustine's Abbey

THE PARSON

RIGHT **After the dissolution the masonry of St Augustine's Abbey was quarried by all and sundry until only the bare bones of the great monastery were left** *in situ*.

BELOW **The Fyndon Gate was the principal entrance into St Augustine's Abbey. Built in 1309, it is the only part of the Abbey which survives intact.**

King Ethelbert proved to be immensely generous to St Augustine after his conversion to Christianity. Not only did he give land within the Roman walls to found the Cathedral and abbey of Christ Church, but he also encouraged St Augustine to set up another great Benedictine abbey just outside the walls to the east of the Cathedral. This Abbey, at first

dedicated to SS Peter and Paul, became the burial place of kings and archbishops, and soon acquired a reputation as a centre of scholarship, renowned for the illuminated manuscripts produced by its monks. In 978, Archbishop Dunstan, who was later canonized himself, re-dedicated the Abbey in the name of its founder whose shrine attracted many pilgrims and benefactions.

The Norman, Lanfranc, was appointed Archbishop of Canterbury in 1070 and not only began rebuilding the Cathedral, but also re-organised the lives of St Augustine's monks and created a more rigorous regime. He appointed a fellow Frenchman, Scolland, as abbot who found the rambling Saxon monastery on the point of collapse. Work began immediately on a new abbey and continued for many years after Abbot Scolland's death in 1087. With income from 12,000 acres (4,860 hectares) of land, St Augustine's was one of the wealthiest Benedictine monasteries in England, reaching its zenith around the time of an earthquake in 1382 which caused damage to the church.

When Henry VIII's commissioners dissolved St Augustine's in 1538, the Abbey housed only 30 monks. Its treasures, including 2,000 books, were dispersed (just 200 volumes from the library survive today) and work began on converting the abbot's lodging into a royal palace so that Henry's new bride, Anne of Cleves (his fourth wife) could stay there on her journey from the continent. Much of the dismantled masonry from other parts of the Abbey were shipped to France and used in the construction of defence works at Calais. Although Henry stayed at Canterbury on a number of further occasions and both Queen Elizabeth I and King Charles I made ceremonial visits, the palace decayed and passed into private ownership,

ABOVE These remarkable roof bosses were rescued from the ruins of the Abbey and date from the 12th century.

part of it becoming a brewery in 1826 owned by William Beer, who laid out pleasure grounds in the surrounding gardens and park. Victorian sensibilities were disturbed by this use, and when the brewery came up for sale in 1844 it was purchased by a benefactor who was instrumental in

founding a missionary college. The college closed in 1947 and its buildings are now used by King's School. The remains of the Abbey are cared for by English Heritage and, along with the Cathedral and St Martin's Church, were declared a World Heritage Site in 1989.

RIGHT Queen Elizabeth I celebrated her 40th birthday whilst staying at St Augustine's Abbey. This image of her is the wonderful Armada Portrait (on display at Woburn Abbey in Bedfordshire).

Thomas Becket

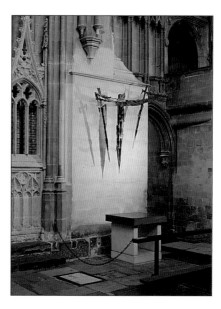

THE CLERK

Born in 1118, the son of a London merchant, Becket was noticed by Theobald, Archbishop of Canterbury, and entered his household. He was, at that time, adviser to the archbishop at the Council of Rheims, who made him Archdeacon of Canterbury and recommended him to Henry II, who was beginning a campaign aimed at restoring the power of the monarchy over the Church. Becket quickly became Henry's favourite and was made chancellor. He played a major part in advancing the influence of the crown

ABOVE **The Altar of the Sword's Point stands in the north transept of the Cathedral near the place where Archbishop Thomas Becket was killed.**

until he was appointed Archbishop of Canterbury in 1161.

Seldom can a man have changed his policies so completely as Becket, who now began a dogged opposition to the king taking over the privileges of the Church. Matters came to a head in 1163 when Becket was charged with treason and had to flee the country. His exile lasted for seven years while arguments raged between Archbishop, Pope and Monarch and the assets of Christ Church Abbey and Canterbury Cathedral were poured into state coffers. In June 1170, a half-hearted compromise was worked out between Henry and Becket, and the latter hurried back to England to make sure that the Church was not completely overwhelmed by the power of the state. In this he had the support of the common people, but was opposed by clergy as well as government. He even found the monks of Canterbury against him and had to replace their prior. Meanwhile, news had come to the king while he was in France that Becket was at large

Geoffrey Chaucer, 'The Father of English Poetry' was born in London *c*.1340. For a short time his father was a butler in the royal household, and with his help Chaucer eventually rose to become the 'dearly beloved valet' of Edward III. The king sent him on missions abroad through which he became familiar with the literature of France and Italy. When Richard II came to the throne, Chaucer briefly lost his influence at court and this allowed him time to write *The Canterbury Tales* which he began *c*.1387 but never finished. He died on 25 October 1400 and was buried in Westminster Abbey, the first poet to lie in what has since become Poets' Corner.

LEFT **A reconstruction of the medieval painting showing the murder of Thomas Becket. The defaced original can be seen at the tomb of King Henry IV.**

RIGHT The Canterbury Pilgrims, painted by Thomas Stothard R.A. in 1817 and on display at the Royal Museum Art Gallery.

CANTERBURY MUSEUMS COLLECTION ©

ABOVE The murder of Thomas Becket is shown in this boss from the nave vaulting of Exeter Cathedral, *c*.1340. It shows how quickly his fame spread to all corners of the kingdom.

in Kent, possibly gathering an army, and on Christmas Day Henry raged to his courtiers that they had allowed a low-born clerk to treat him with contempt. Four of his knights took this to be a royal command and sailed to England intending to arrest Becket.

When the knights confronted him in the Cathedral on 29 December, he defied them with quiet faith and courage until, resisting their attempts to drag him from the Cathedral, they were provoked into using their swords. A monk, Edward Grim, tried to fend off the first blow, but the heavy sword almost cut through his arm and landed on Becket's head, cutting away his scalp. Becket remained standing, his head bowed, until further blows to his head brought him to his knees and he said: 'For the name of Jesus and the

defence of the Church, I am ready to embrace death'. At this, to share responsibility, each of the knights struck again at Becket's head and fled, leaving him with the crown of his head split from the skull (hence the significance of the Corona built later at the east end of the Cathedral, see p.15).

Becket's death was a pivotal event of the age. Almost immediately he was acclaimed as a martyr and his relics were venerated for healing incurable diseases. The king was filled with guilt and remorse for his murder and in 1174 came to Canterbury to be scourged at Becket's tomb by the 80 monks of the Cathedral's Abbey. The Church retained its independence from the monarch until Henry VIII established the Protestant faith in 1536.

RIGHT This 13th-century portrait of St Thomas Becket is in one of the windows which overlooked his shrine in Trinity Chapel at the eastern end of the Cathedral.

FAR RIGHT King Henry II, St Thomas Becket's one-time friend, bitterly regretted his rash and hasty words which led to the archbishop's murder.

KING HENRY THE II.

Churches and friaries

At the height of the city's medieval prosperity, there were 22 churches within the city walls, while St Dunstan's and St Martin's stood a short distance outside. Of all Canterbury's churches, **St Martin's** holds the most interest. It is almost certainly the church where Queen Bertha worshipped before the arrival of St Augustine, and Roman bricks were used in both the nave and chancel which also both display Saxon features. On the opposite side of the city **St Mildred's**, close to the castle, also has Roman tiles in its masonry and even though it was damaged by fire in 1246, enough remains to show that townsfolk were worshipping here in Saxon times.

Holy Cross Church was originally situated over the West Gate, but was rebuilt adjacent to a new gate erected by Archbishop Sudbury *c.*1375. It contrasts with the gate, is built of dark flint rather than light ragstone, and now serves Canterbury as the council chamber. **St Peter's Church** lies closer to the city centre, an endearing little building tucked behind houses scarcely younger than itself – it dates

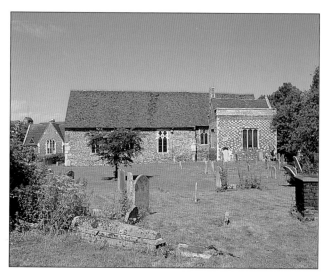

BELOW St Mildred was a Saxon princess who became a nun and died *c.*700. She was canonised and St Augustine's Abbey held her shrine and relics. The church which bears her name stands in a grassy churchyard near the Castle.

FAR LEFT St Martin's lies outside the city walls close to Canterbury prison and is the city's oldest church. It is probable that Queen Bertha worshipped at St Martin's before her husband, King Ethelbert, was converted by St Augustine.

LEFT Old gravestones can still be seen in the former churchyard of Holy Cross Church.

from Norman times, though most of it is early 14th century. The interior is surprisingly spacious, with old-fashioned features.

Two other churches, like Holy Cross, now serve secular purposes. At the heart of the city **St Margaret's** now houses an audio-visual experience describing the **Canterbury Tales**. The church was restored in the 19th century after its chancel had been drastically truncated to enable stagecoaches to use the street. The 12th-century **St Alphege's**, in Palace Street, is now the Canterbury Environment Centre where the work of Canterbury craftsmen is on display.

Within 50 years of Becket's death (when St Francis was still alive) **Franciscans** (Greyfriars) established a house in Canterbury, their first in England. All that remains is a small, two-storey building which straddles the river behind the Poor Priests' Hospital (The Heritage Museum). Surrounded by a wild-flower meadow, this is the most charming of Canterbury's hidden treasures where Eucharist is celebrated during the summer at lunchtime on Wednesdays.

Further downstream, the **Dominican** (Blackfriars) house also spanned the river. The refectory built in 1260 survives, as do fragments of the guest hall on the opposite side of the Stour. The **Augustinians** (Whitefriars) were the third of the major orders to settle in Canterbury. Their church was situated near St George's and was destroyed by bombs in 1942, although the name lives on with the Whitefriars shopping centre which now covers the site.

Robert Cushman was a Canterbury grocer's assistant who had a key role in the Pilgrim Fathers' voyage to America in 1620. He negotiated the charter of the *Mayflower* at a house in Palace Street. He and his family eventually reached America aboard the *Fortune* in 1621. Palace Street was the home of Phillipe de la Noye, who sailed with Cushman on the *Fortune*. Once settled in New Plymouth, he changed his name to Delano. President Franklin Delano Roosevelt was his descendant.

ABOVE St Peter's gives its name to one of Canterbury's principal thoroughfares. Many thousands of pilgrims must have trudged past this unassuming flint church which is still regularly used for services.

LEFT St Margaret's Church now houses The Canterbury Tales audio-visual experience.

RIGHT This little building by the River Stour is all that survives of the Greyfriars (Franciscan) monastery dating from 1267.

Historic buildings

THE SQUIRE

A handful of buildings make Canterbury famous as a medieval city, but its character depends on the hundreds of more humble houses which give the streets their charm and beauty. Not all of these homes are medieval or Tudor – if you venture away from the crowds in the heart of the city, you will discover gracious Georgian town houses as well as streets of early Victorian terraced cottages with their own cosy, well-preserved appeal. Many of Canterbury's most ancient buildings are disguised by fronts added in the days when age was not held to be an asset to a property. Vertical 'mathematical' tiling was a popular way of giving old buildings a new look in the 19th century so that they appeared to be built of brick – there are some good examples of this in the High Street and Butter Market.

Over the centuries, most of the city's ancient houses have changed their purpose as well as their appearance. The **Old Weavers' Houses** which overlook Eastbridge or, more correctly, the King's Bridge at the northern end of High Street, are no exception. They stand at the heart of Canterbury where the first huts of the original settlement were built. In the 12th century, there was a large hall-house on the site and some of this structure survives, although it is hidden among later fabrics. In the mid-16th century, Huguenot refugees adapted the medieval house so that its large windows lit the looms at which they worked. The low Norman doorway on the opposite side of the street leads into **Eastbridge Hospital**, which was originally a hospice for travellers but became a pilgrims'

Charles Dickens is known to have stayed at the Sun Inn when he visited Canterbury in the 19th century, but he is chiefly associated with one of the most beautiful of the city's timber-framed buildings – the House of Agnes in St Dunstan's. This was the 'very old house bulging out over the road' in *David Copperfield* where the young hero lodged with the Wickfields whilst at Dr Strong's school.

ABOVE LEFT The 15th-century building known as Queen Elizabeth's Guest Chamber was once the Crown Inn but there is little evidence that the Virgin Queen was ever its patron. The bacchanalian cupids were added to its front in 1663.

LEFT The 12th-century undercroft of Eastbridge Hospital, founded before 1180.

RIGHT One of the grotesque wooden figures which decorate the Tudor House in Palace Street.

FAR RIGHT Sir John Boys' House on the corner where Palace Street meets King Street has a famous leaning doorway. The house tilted when an internal chimney was altered.

BELOW Conquest House is built above a Norman cellar where Thomas Becket's murderers are supposed to have gathered before crossing the road to confront the archbishop. Its Tudor façade disguises a medieval house.

hostel before 1180. Its outstanding undercroft and hall date from this time though the chapel, with its crown-post roof, is late 14th-century.

Nearby, in the High Street, **Queen Elizabeth's Guest Chamber** is often said to be the best medieval timber-framed structure within the city walls. Its name is misleading, since the Queen lodged at the royal palace at St Augustine's for her visit in 1573, and at the time the Chamber was part of the Crown Inn. However, the building does have historical importance as it was the venue for the Queen's meeting with an unsuccessful suitor, the Duc d'Alençon, the son of Catherine de Medici, Queen of France. The exterior plasterwork has a pair of tipsy-looking cherubs sitting on barrels among grape-vines.

Palace Street has an exceptional array of old houses, even though its buildings are mostly on the west side, facing the Archbishop's Palace from which it takes its name. Moving northwards from Sun Street, the **Tudor House** (also known as **St Alphege's Priest's House**) is the first one to note, with fearsome beasts carved on brackets supporting the overhang. Further along, **Conquest House** is now an antiques shop, but its Norman undercroft is supposed to be where the knights met before entering the Cathedral to murder Becket. There are several more attractive buildings along this street as well as **Sir John Boys' House** on the corner. With its skewed door and a tilt which could rival Pisa's, this must be one of the most photographed houses in the kingdom. Sir John Boys was the first Recorder of Canterbury and served five archbishops in his position of High Steward.

On the opposite side of town, just inside the city walls, stand the remains of the Norman **Castle**. Its masonry suffered badly from years of use as a coke store and all of its facing stone has gone.

Museums and galleries

THE WIFE
OF BATH

Canterbury's four museums are situated in the city centre and provide a comprehensive introduction to the city's history and development.

The **Museum of Canterbury**, in Stour Street, occupies a medieval flint building which in its time has served as home of a notoriously greedy, 12th-century moneylender, Poor Priests' Hospital, a workhouse and an orphanage. Recently renovated, the museum has something for everyone, offering many interactive exhibits, including a wartime Blitz experience and medieval discovery gallery, illustrating the history of Canterbury from the earliest settlements to the end of the last century. There are galleries and displays devoted to those connected with Canterbury as

diverse as Rupert Bear, author Joseph Conrad and cartoon characters Bagpuss and The Clangers.

The Roman era is covered in detail at the **Roman Museum** in Butchery Lane. Visitors descend to the level of a 2nd-century street and can see reconstructions of the shops in the market place and the apartments of the large town house which once stood on this site. A fine mosaic floor miraculously survived over-building and the bombing of 1942 and this provides the highlight of the exhibition. Young visitors will enjoy playing the games which amused Roman children 1,600 years ago and handling real artefacts in a 'touch the past' experience.

The **West Gate**, dating from *c.*1375, is the most impressive surviving feature of the city's ancient defences. The only one of the eight original gates, it has survived mainly because it served as Canterbury's gaol from the 15th century until 1829. There is a grand view of the city from the battlements which project in places so that defenders could pour hot liquids on their enemies. The small museum tells the tale of Canterbury's more

BELOW
This beautiful Saxon pendant, discovered in 1982, is on display in the Museum of Canterbury. The gold cross is surrounded by an intricate setting of garnets.

RIGHT
The Museum of Canterbury is in Stour Street and occupies what was the Poor Priests' Hospital, a medieval flint building which still has its crown-post roof.

CANTERBURY MUSEUMS COLLECTION ©

CANTERBURY MUSFILMS COLLECTION ©

ABOVE The *Invicta*, built by Stephenson in 1830 for the Canterbury and Whitstable Railway, in the Museum of Canterbury.

CANTERBURY MUSEUMS COLLECTION ©

RIGHT
The Roman Museum's mosaic floor can be seen *in situ*, **and many other artefacts are also on view.**

Mary Tourtel, creator of the famous bear, Rupert, was born in Canterbury at 51 Palace Street, on 28 January 1874. The first cartoon strip appeared in the *Daily Express* on 8 November 1920 and Rupert has remained a popular feature of the newspaper ever since. Tourtel married a night editor on the *Express* who was also a poet, and it followed that she drew the illustrations while he wrote the verses below. A momentous change occurred in the 1930s when Rupert began to wear a red jumper rather than the former blue one. Over the years a succession of artists have depicted Rupert's adventures.

RIGHT Visitors to the West Gate Mueum can climb to the battlements to see this view of the city.

violent past exhibiting arms and armour as well as items such as manacles and the old gallows, relics of the time when the gate served as the gaol.

The **Royal Museum and Art Gallery** occupies the first floor of the half-timbered Beaney Institute in the High Street. Mr Beaney was a native of Canterbury who made a fortune in Australia and in 1897 paid for the building to house the library, museum and art gallery. Today the museum's galleries display the city's collection of paintings. One of the galleries is devoted to the Victorian painter, Thomas Sidney Cooper, who lived in Canterbury and was famous for his studies of cattle, while another is dedicated to special exhibitions. Examples of porcelain and other fine decorative art, many by local craftsmen, are also on display. The museum of the local regiment, the Buffs (which was amalgamated into

The Queen's Regiment in 1966), shares the premises and testifies to a long and glorious history. Entrance to the Royal Museum and Art Gallery is free.

The **Canterbury Tales Visitor Attraction** is located in the medieval St Margaret's Church in St Margaret's Street. This audio-visual experience allows visitors to join Geoffrey Chaucer's band of medieval pilgrims on their journey from London's Tabard Inn to the shrine of St Thomas Becket in Canterbury Cathedral. The latest technology provides the sights, sounds and even smells of 14th-century England, while the pilgrims tell their tales, some tragic, others comical. Commentary is supplied in six languages in addition to English, and there is also a children's version (though this is in English only).

BELOW The imposing Victorian façade of the Royal Museum and Art Gallery.

Further information

THE COOK

Visitor Information Centre

The Centre carries a wide range of information about Canterbury and the local area, and includes a shop. Helpful and friendly staff are on hand to answer queries, book accommodation, excursions, and tickets for local events, plus for London Theatres. *12/13 Sun Street, The Buttermarket. Open Easter–Oct Mon–Sat 09.30–17.00, Sun 10.00–16.00; Oct–Easter Mon–Sat 10.00–16.00. Closed Sun, Jan-Mar. Tel: 01227 378100 www.canterbury.co.uk*

Canterbury Cathedral

The magnificent, medieval Cathedral is part of the Canterbury World Heritage Site. Photography for private purposes is allowed in the Cathedral, except in the Crypt, provided a permit is purchased first. Last entry is 30 minutes before closing. *Open for general visiting: Sundays throughout the year: 12.30–14.30 & 16.30–17.30; Easter–end Sep Mon–Sat 09.00–18.30, Mon in termtime 09.00–17.30; Oct–Easter Mon–Sat 09.00–17.00. The Crypt: Easter–end Sep Mon–Sun 10.00–18.30; Oct–Easter Mon–Sun 10.00–17.00. Visitors may be requested to leave during the last half-hour of opening times or before the beginning of a service. Access is restricted during services. Audio and guided tours are available in several languages. Guided tours take place at regular intervals throughout the day. Admission charges to the Precinct apply at certain times. Tel: 01227 762862. www.canterbury-cathedral.org*

Services

Sundays
Holy Communion: 08.00
Matins (either said or sung by King's School): 09.30
Sung Eucharist with sermon: 11.00
Choral Evensong: 15.15
Evening service with sermon: 18.30.
Weekdays
Holy Communion: 08.00 (also Wed 10.15 or 11.00; Thur 18.15, Major Saints' Days [sung] 10.15)
Matins: 07.30 Mon–Fri in the Chapel of Our Lady Martyrdom; Sat 09.30 in the Jesus Chapel
The Thursday Candle – Prayer for Unity in the Chapel of Our Lady Undercroft: 15.30
Choral Evensong 17.30 (Sat 15.15).

Canterbury Environment Centre

Situated in the converted medieval St Alphege's Church, the Centre promotes awareness of the city through exhibitions. *St Alphege Lane, off Palace Street. Open Tues–Fri 10.00–17.00, Sat 10.00–16.00. Small admission fee. Tel: 01227 457009 www.canterburycentre.org.uk*

The Canterbury Tales

The 14th century is recreated to depict the world of poet Geoffrey Chaucer and the journey of the Canterbury Pilgrims from London to Canterbury Cathedral. *St Margaret's Street. Open daily, usually 09.30–17.00. Admission charge. Tel: 01227 479227 www.canterburytales.org.uk*

Eastbridge Hospital

An early medieval pilgrims' hostel with Norman undercroft, refectory with early 13th-century mural and Pilgrims' Chapel. *High Street. Open Mon–Sat 10.00–17.00. Admission charge. Tel: 01227 471688 www.eastbridgehospital.org.uk*

BELOW **Unusual tree-sculptures in Solly's Orchard near St Radigund's Bridge.**

BELOW LEFT **The Tourist Information Centre is situated in Sun Street.**

ABOVE **Buskers playing in High Street during the summer.**

RIGHT **The Stour flows through colourful Westgate Gardens, given to the city in 1936.**

Greyfriars Chapel

This picturesque Franciscan building, constructed during the lifetime of St Francis of Assisi, spans the River Stour.
Off Stour Street (to the right as you approach Museum of Canterbury from High Street). Open Easter–end Sep Mon–Sat 14.00–16.00. Eucharist service 12.30 every Wed. Donations welcome.
Tel: 01227 471688
www.canterbury.co.uk

Museum of Canterbury

A 21st century museum, which guarantees visitors have fun discovering Canterbury's history through exciting displays and hands-on activities.
Stour Street. Open daily Mon–Sat 10.30–17.00 and Jun–Oct Sun 13.30–17.00 (last entry one hour before closing times). Admission charge. Tel: 01227 475202
www.canterbury-museums.co.uk

Roman Museum

Set below street level, this museum has a preserved town house with original mosaic floors and reconstructed marketplace.
Longmarket, Butchery Lane. Open daily 10.30–17.00 and June–Oct Sun 13.30–17.00. Last entry one hour before closing times. Admission charge.
Tel: 01227 785575
www.canterbury-museums.co.uk

Royal Museum and Art Gallery & Buffs Regimental Museum

There are fine permanent exhibitions of porcelain and paintings. The Buffs Regimental Museum exhibits the stirring history of the famous regiment.
High Street. Open Mon–Sat 10.00–17.00. Tel: 01227 452747
www.canterbury-artgallery.co.uk

St Augustine's Abbey

Free audio tours available to explore the Abbey ruins.
Longport. Open Apr–Sep 10.00–18.00, Oct 10.00–17.00, Nov–Mar 10.00–16.00. Admission charge. Tel: 01227 767345
www.english-heritage.org.uk

BELOW **The medieval chapel of Eastbridge Hospital.**

Tours round Canterbury

Look round Canterbury by boat, punt, horse-drawn carriage or bicycle, or take a Ghost Tour. The Canterbury Guild of Guides leads daily walks lasting about 1½ hours from April to October from the Tourist Information Centre. A variety of languages is on offer.

West Gate Towers

As well as wonderful views from the battlements, exhibits illustrating the gate's eventful history are on display. Children can try on replica armour and you can make your own brass rubbings.
St Peter's Street. Open daily Mon–Sat 1100–12.30 and 13.30–15.30. Last entry 15 minutes before closing times. Admission charge.
Tel: 01227 789576
www.canterbury.co.uk

Festivals
Canterbury Cricket Festival

Early Aug: one week of cricket at the St Lawrence Ground.
Tel: 01227 456886 for fixtures

Canterbury Festival

Mid-Oct: a two-week mixed arts festival with productions ranging from large-scale opera to local community events.
Tel: 01227 452853
www.canterburyfestival.co.uk